21st Century
Junior Library

TALKING ABOUT GENDER

AnneMarie McClain and Lacey Hilliard

Topics to Talk About

Published in the United States of America by Cherry Lake Publishing Group
Ann Arbor, Michigan
www.cherrylakepublishing.com

Reading Adviser: Beth Walker Gambro, MS, Ed., Reading Consultant, Yorkville, IL
Book Designer: Jen Wahi

Photo Credits: Cover: © Yulyazolotko/Shutterstock; page 5: © Pond Saksit/Shutterstock; page 6: © EZ-Stock Studio/Shutterstock; page 7: © Jacob Lund/Shutterstock; page 8: © BearFotos/Shutterstock; page 10–11: © Monkey Business Images/Shutterstock; page 12 (left): © PlutusART/Shutterstock; page 12 (right): © Monkey Business Images/Shutterstock; page 13: © fizkes/Shutterstock; page 14: © Rawpixel.com/Shutterstock; page 15 (top): © Monkey Business Images/Shutterstock; page 15 (bottom left): © ibragimova/Shutterstock; page 15 (bottom right): © spass/Shutterstock; page 16: © Sofarina79/Shutterstock; page 18: © Robert Kneschke/Shutterstock; page 19: © Pixel-Shot/Shutterstock; page 20 (left): © Lucky Business/Shutterstock; page 20 (right): © Samuel Borges Photography/Shutterstock; page 21: © BKHRB/Shutterstock

Library of Congress Cataloging-in-Publication Data

Names: Hilliard, Lacey, author. | McClain, AnneMarie, author.
Title: Talking about gender / written by: Lacey Hilliard and AnneMarie McClain.
Description: Ann Arbor, Michigan : Cherry Lake Publishing, [2023] | Series: Topics to talk about | Audience: Grades 2-3 | Summary: "How do we talk about gender? This book breaks down the topic of gender for young readers. Filled with engaging photos and captions, this series opens up opportunities for deeper thought and informed conversation. Guided exploration of topics in 21st Century Junior Library's signature style help readers to Look, Think, Ask Questions, Make Guesses, and Create as they go!"– Provided by publisher.
Identifiers: LCCN 2022039651 | ISBN 9781668919361 (hardcover) | ISBN 9781668920381 (paperback) | ISBN 9781668923047 (pdf) | ISBN 9781668921715 (ebook)
Subjects: LCSH: Gender identity–Juvenile literature. | Gender identity in children–Juvenile literature. | Gender nonconformity–Juvenile literature.
Classification: LCC HQ1075 .H535 2023 | DDC 305–dc23/eng/20220818
LC record available at https://lccn.loc.gov/2022039651

Cherry Lake Publishing would like to acknowledge the work of the Partnership for 21st Century Learning, a network of Battelle for Kids. Please visit http://www.battelleforkids.org/networks/p21 for more information.

Printed in the United States of America
Corporate Graphics

CHERRY LAKE PRESS

CONTENTS

Let's Talk About Gender   4

Kids and Gender   8

What's Most Important
to Remember?   21

Reflecting About Gender   21

Glossary   22
Learn More   23
Index   24
About the Authors   24

LET'S TALK ABOUT GENDER

Gender is a part of who people are.

There are girls, boys, nonbinary people, Two-Spirit people, and other genders. Some people whose gender changes call themselves gender fluid. For some people, it feels best to say they have no gender.

Transgender is a word for when grown-ups guessed wrong about someone's gender when they were born.

There are many different genders. There isn't just girl or boy.

5

A transgender girl is someone who everyone thought was a boy but is actually a girl. A transgender boy is someone who everyone thought was a girl but is actually a boy.

Cisgender is a word for when grown-ups guessed right about someone's gender when they were born.

Some cisgender kids feel strongly about their gender. So do transgender kids!

A cisgender girl is someone who everyone thought was a girl and is a girl. A cisgender boy is someone who everyone thought was a boy and is a boy.

Each person can choose which words feel right for their gender. You can even pick your own new words for gender. Everyone can change their gender words, too. People are who they say they are.

7

8

Ask Questions!

Have you heard these gender words before? What questions do you have after learning about genders?

Pronouns are a part of gender. Pronouns are words like she/her, they/them, and he/they. When someone figures out their gender, they may say which pronouns are best for them. Pronouns can change. If you don't know someone's pronouns, that's okay. You can ask if they'd feel comfortable telling you. You can use their name. You can use the word "you."

You can't tell someone's gender or pronouns just by looking at them. Some people think some clothes, toys, and jobs are only for one gender. That is not true. Thinking something is only for one gender is called a stereotype. All clothes, toys, sports, games, and jobs are for all genders.

KIDS AND GENDER

What do you know about gender? Have you thought much about gender?

You may already have your gender figured out. You might not have thought much about gender. You may be still thinking about it. This is all okay. You also don't have to figure it out.

People can have big feelings or say things about gender.

Make a Guess

What would the world be like if no one ever said gender stereotypes are wrong? What would it feel like?

Gender is something each person figures out for themselves. You can always learn about yourself and other people. Kids can help teach grown-ups, too. Sometimes kids are the best teachers.

Treating others with kindness and compassion is the most important thing!

Books, TV shows, videos, and movies do not always show genders other than boys and girls. This can be frustrating because there are people with many other genders. Kids of all genders should be seen. They are all important.

Kids of all genders should be seen and treated with kindness and respect.

If a friend trusts you, they may choose to share thoughts they are having about gender. If you don't know what to say, listening is always important.

WHAT'S MOST IMPORTANT TO REMEMBER?

Gender can be an important part of who people are. The way people think about their gender can change. Gender can also take time to figure out.

Think!

What would you say if a friend told you they weren't sure about their gender? If you aren't sure what you would say, who could you ask for help?

It might sometimes seem like there are only boys and girls, but that's not true. There are many different genders. No gender is better than any other gender. Kids of all genders are important. You should feel good about who you are. There are wonderful kids with all kinds of genders out there in the world. Some are just like you!

Kids of all genders are important.

Some people think certain things are "only for girls" or "only for boys." They are thinking with gender stereotypes.

REFLECTING ABOUT GENDER

Think about someone you love. What is that person's gender? Do you know that person's gender? Do you know that person's pronouns? If you're not sure about pronouns, that's okay. You can ask them if they'd like to tell you or use the person's name or the word "you."

What can you do to make sure kids of all genders feel included at your school? What is something the grown-ups can do to make sure kids of all genders feel **included** at your school?

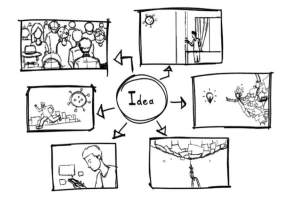

There are some things that people say are "only for girls" or "only for boys." What do you think about this?

Do you think people of all genders feel included in your community? If not, what are some things you could do to help?

Create!

Come up with a TV show or book idea with your friends. Think of a plan that would help all kids feel seen.

GLOSSARY

cisgender (siss-JEHN-duhr) person who identifies as the gender assigned at birth

gender (JEHN-duhr) a person's self-perception of who they are or inner feeling as boy, girl, another gender, and/or something else

gender fluid (JEHN-duhr FLOO-uhd) gender identity that isn't fixed

included (in-KLOO-duhd) made to feel part of a group

nonbinary (nahn-BY-nuh-ree) gender identity that does not fall into the gender binary groups of male or female

pronouns (PROH-nowns) words that refer to someone in place of their name

stereotype (STEHR-ee-oh-typ) view that all people in a certain group act and think the same

transgender (trahns-JEHN-duhr) person who is not the gender they were assigned at birth

Two-Spirit (TOO-SPIHR-uht) is a word that someone who is Indigenous, First Nations, or Native American might use to describe themselves when their gender identity does not fall into the gender binary groups of male or female, or is one that falls outside of the Western notions of gender

LEARN MORE

Book: *It Feels Good to Be Yourself* by Theresa Thorn (2019) https://us.macmillan.com/books/9781250302953/itfeelsgoodtobeyourself

Book: *The Gender Wheel* by Maya Gonzalez (2010) https://reflectionpress.com/our-books/the-gender-wheel

INDEX

cisgender people, 6–7

gender fluid people, 4
genders, 4–5, 10, 12, 14, 18
gender stereotypes, 9, 11, 19, 21

identity, 7, 9, 12, 17, 20
inclusion, 14, 21

language, 7, 9, 20

media messages, 14

nonbinary people, 4

pronouns, 9, 20

representation, 14, 21

stereotypes, 9, 11, 19, 21

transgender people, 4, 6
Two-Spirit people, 4

words, 7, 9, 20

ABOUT THE AUTHORS

AnneMarie K. McClain is an educator, researcher, and parent. Her work is about how kids and families can feel good about who they are. She especially loves finding ways to help kids and families feel seen in TV and books.

Lacey J. Hilliard is a college professor, researcher, and parent. Her work is in understanding how grown-ups talk to children about the world around them. She particularly likes hearing what kids have to say about things.